# My Horse, My Friend

## Hands-On TTouch® Training for Kids

Bibi Degn

with photos by
Horst Streitferdt

Translated by
Lilliana Joseph



T
TRAFALGAR SQUARE
North Pomfret, Vermont

First published in 2011 by
Trafalgar Square Books
North Pomfret, Vermont 05053

**Printed in China**

Originally published in the German language as *Mein Pferd, mein Freund* by Franckh-Kosmos Verlags-GmbH & Co. KG, Stuttgart

Copyright © 2010 Franckh-Kosmos Verlags-GmbH & Co. KG, Stuttgart
English translation © 2011 Trafalgar Square Books

**Library of Congress Cataloging-in-Publication Data**

Degn, Bibi.

My horse, my friend : hands-on touch training for kids / Bibi Degn. p. cm.

 Summary: "Through the charming story of Maike and her budding relationship with her Arab gelding Joram, this handbook teaches kids how to properly interact with horses. Together with Maike, young equestrians will find out how to successfully greet, lead, groom, and mount a horse, and learn relationship-strengthening obstacle games to play on the ground and on horseback. Horse-loving kids will master essential skills for engaging with horses while also discovering the exhilaration and excitement of horse companionship"—Provided by publisher.

 Summary: "A step-by-step guide to showing kids how to communicate with and handle a horse in a way that respects the horse and keeps the child safe"—Provided by publisher.

 ISBN 978-1-57076-481-3 (hardback)

 1. Horses--Training--Juvenile literature.  I. Title.

 SF287.D44 2011

 636.1--dc22

2011006205

Cover design by RM Didier

All photographs are by Horst Streitferdt/Kosmos, Stuttgart except for the photographs on page 11 (above) and page 27 (above left), which are by Lothar Lenz, Kosmos.

Illustrations by Petra Eimer

Typefaces: ITC Charter, Cronos NM, Matrix Script

10 9 8 7 6 5 4 3 2 1

# Contents

 Maria, Joram ... *6*

 ... and Angie *8*

 TheTTouches *10*

 Leading *12*

 Grooming and TTouch *14*

 Seeing and Feeling *16*

 Leading with a Partner *18*

# Contents *continued*

Riding Bareback ... *20*

Neck Ring and Obstacles *22*

Riding with a Saddle *24*

In the Labyrinth *26*

After the Ride *28*

Parts of the Horse *30*

Goodbye! *31*

# Hello!

This picture shows everyone who helped to make this book. I am Bibi, the author and a riding instructor. Next to me are Olivia, Joram (a lovely gray horse), Olli, and Maria. Flying above us is the most important character in the pages ahead: Angie.

Angie is the "guardian angel" of animals. She appeared when I decided to write about how children and horses can become best friends.

Angie knows what horses want. She whispered many things to me and I typed what she said. Then Olivia, Olli, Maria, and Joram helped us create photographs so you can understand what I've tried to explain with words. That is how we all worked together to create this book, and we really hope you enjoy it!

*Bibi*

# Maria, *Joram* ...

## Angie, the "Guardian Angel" of Animals

Maria has seen Angie a lot in her dreams. Angie is the guardian angel of all animals. Angie is very tiny and lively—like a dragonfly dancing in the sunlight.

Today Maria needs Angie's help. She would like to make friends with the shy white Arabian horse named Joram, but Joram is afraid of people. How can Maria find Angie now that she needs her?

## Maria Asks the Animals for Help

Maria goes up to the bird that is perched on the horses' water trough. Maria asks him, "How can I find Angie?" The bird answers, "You have to fly!" But Maria can't fly.

Next, Maria asks Elia, the happy dog that lives on the farm, where she can find Angie. Elia loves to frolic in the fields and thinks her black and white spots are beautiful. Elia says, "I don't know what you mean—you don't need Angie, you have me!"

Maria finds Joana, the wise old cat, and asks her. Joana listens and says, "Hmm…" then waits for a moment and again says, "Hmm!" She begins to purr and at first Maria can't make out another word.

## Maria Learns to Listen

Maria lays her hands on Joana's fur and feels its softness. Maria puts her ear up to the gnarly old pear tree and listens to it grow. She feels the warm wind upon her skin, and hears whispering all around her. Now she isn't thinking anymore, just feeling.

Suddenly, out of the warm wind, out of the bark of the old pear tree, and out of Joana's soft fur comes a joyful ringing, giggling, jingling, a playful laugh, an aroma, and a caress—and then there she is: Angie, the tiny guardian angel of animals.

Angie lands trustingly on the palm of Maria's hand. She hardly weighs anything. Angie says, "Come on, Maria. You and I and Elia the happy dog will go to find Joram, the shy, white horse."

## Maria Sits in the Garden and Waits

Joana comes and sits on Maria's lap with a thoughtful expression on her face. "Angie wants to help you," she says after a while. "You can find her. You must clear your head of all thoughts." So Maria sets aside all her thoughts, as well as all the things for which she wishes.

But then new thoughts appear. Maria pushes them away. And when a new wish enters her mind she sends it away, too. One of Maria's friends comes over to play, and with her arrive new thoughts and wishes. All day long, Maria pushes away her thoughts and wishes, and they gather in a pile until there is a huge mountain of good, bad, friendly, cheerful, and sad thoughts and wishes under the pear tree.

Maria's biggest wish, of course, is to find Angie! How can she push this one away with all the others?

Joana comes to Maria again. She says, "You have to be curious with all your senses: Feel with your skin and your fingers, smell with your nose, and hear with your ears!"

# ... and Angie

Angie sits snugly in Maria's hand and allows Maria to carry her out to Joram's field. Elia bounds along beside them—black-and-white-spotted and happy. They find Joram standing in the tall grass, looking shy. The wind blows gently through his mane. His coat has tiny spots that look like freckles. Angie hops out of Maria's hand and lands as softly as a butterfly between the ears of the white horse.

## A Wish Comes True

Angie whispers into Joram's ear. She tells him how much Maria loves him. Maria sits in the grass. Joram comes over to her. He puts his nostril up to Maria's cheek and gently blows her blonde hair away from her face. They remain quietly together for a little while, and later, Maria and her new friend go back to the barn. Joram's head rests on Maria's hand as they walk.

The other people at the barn watch Maria and Joram with wide eyes. The white horse has never let anyone lead him before! Angie rides along happily between Joram's ears and is glad that no one can see her except for Maria.

## How Maria Greets Joram

Every day after that, Maria goes to Joram's pasture and calls to him, even when she is still far away from him. Sometimes she greets him loudly and sometimes

quite softly. Maria always clears her head of all other thoughts—she wants to be completely focused on Joram, just as she was on the first day when she found Angie. When Maria sees her friend with the beautiful mane, she sends away all her thoughts about school and her friends. She makes room just for Joram. Either in her head or out loud, she asks him, "How are you today?" Then, if Maria is quiet for a moment she can hear and feel Angie's little voice, softly telling her how Joram feels.

Only then does Maria walk up to Joram and let him sniff her hand in greeting.

Today Maria's friend Olli is at the barn, too. Together they put a halter and a "zephyr lead rope" on Joram: A zephyr is a "soft breeze," and a zephyr lead rope has a piece of soft cord on one end to use on the horse's sensitive nose. First, Maria lays her hands on Joram's nose and behind his ears so that he will lower his head. Then, Olli puts the lead rope around Joram's neck so he can hold Joram or ask him to keep his head down with the rope so that Maria can put on the halter.

Horses like to have a little bit of room around them. If you stand too close to a horse's head it is just like when someone stands too close to you when talking to you. Joram likes it best when Maria stands half-an-arm-length away, just like she is doing in these photos.

*Maria threads the zephyr lead rope through the metal ring on the side of the halter and crosses it over the noseband.*

*On the other side of Joram's head, Maria pulls the lead rope through the halter ring—from the inside to the outside—and clips it to the halter's upper ring.*

*When the zephyr lead rope is fastened correctly, it crosses over the front of the halter's noseband.*

# The TTouches

Angie and Maria are friends now. Maria envies Angie's beautiful dragonfly wings. Angie admires Maria's hands. Horses love people's hands because their touch can feel so pleasant and comforting. But Angie has little hooves and wings—no hands.

Therefore Angie needs Maria's help. "Joram would like to be touched nicely today, Maria," she says. "Are you familiar with the TTouches?" Maria hasn't heard of TTouch before, but she is eager to learn.

*TTouches on the horse's forehead as a soft greeting create trust.*

TTouches are very specific ways to lay your hands on an animal's body. They are gentle and good for all kinds of animals. You can use TTouches to win your horse's trust and improve his health. Maria lays the palm of her hand gently on Joram's coat and softly rubs it.

"That feels good to Joram—it is a TTouch called the Jellyfish TTouch," says Angie. "Now try moving his skin around in a circle." Maria learns quickly. She puts her fingers on Joram's forehead and softly moves his skin in a small circle.

*The Clouded Leopard TTouch moves the horse's skin clockwise in a circle.*

"TTouch" stands for Tellington Touch, or T-Touch. TTouches were invented by a very famous horse and animal trainer named Linda Tellington-Jones and are a gentle way to communicate with your horse and make him more confident.

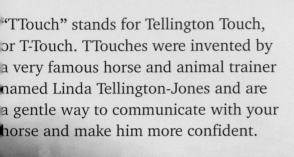

## Linda Tellington-Jones

discovered that people's hands can communicate with animals. This is why Linda invented TTouches and other ways to train with kindness. Linda was the first person to "see" Angie and tell others how to find her, too.

When Joram is afraid of something, he stands with his head up high in the air. Maria must be careful because he could spook—become frightened—and run off. Horses are "flight" animals. "Look, he is your friend, he is lowering his head," whispers Angie very softly so as not to disturb Joram. Maria learns that when horses lower their head it is not because they are sad, but rather because they trust the people around them.

Maria cups her hand on Joram's shoulder as if her whole hand were a sea shell snuggling up against his coat. Joram closes his eyes. This is called the Abalone TTouch.

*The TTouch Circle is the foundation of all other TTouches: With your fingers slightly curved, gently place one hand on the horse. Begin at the bottom of an imaginary circle and push the horse's skin around one entire time, then one-quarter circle more.*

# Leading

Joram is stronger than Maria, but he follows her because they are friends. Maria must "speak" to Joram in a way that he can understand what she wants. First, Maria visualizes Joram doing exactly what she would like him to do, then she "speaks" with her body and with her aids—the zephyr lead rope and the "wand." The wand is a stiff white stick with a plastic "button" on one end, and it is called the wand because the different things you can do with it work like magic.

Elephants have a very flexible trunk. They swing their trunk forward and then back again when they walk. This is exactly how Maria swings the handle end of the wand as she walks with Joram. Leading a horse like this is called the Elegant Elephant: When Maria swings her "trunk" forward, Joram knows that he should follow her and when she swings it backward, he should slow or come to a stop.

Maria carries the wand with the handle pointing forward to "point" to where she wants Joram to go.

Angie sweeps her dragonfly wings softly over Maria's arm. "See how nice the touch of my wings feels?" she says. "You should stroke Joram's legs often with the wand, lightly, like my wings on your arm. It's best to start higher and move down toward his hooves."

*In all the pictures in this book you can see that Maria never wraps the lead rope around her hand. That would be dangerous. She always carries the rope in loops in her hand.*

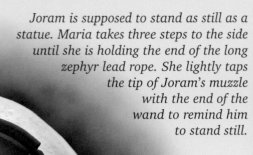

*Joram is supposed to stand as still as a statue. Maria takes three steps to the side until she is holding the end of the long zephyr lead rope. She lightly taps the tip of Joram's muzzle with the end of the wand to remind him to stand still.*

When Maria wants Joram to halt, she points the wand at his chest and taps him lightly. This is the signal to halt. She holds the lead rope with one hand right near the halter and lifts the other hand with the extra loops. In a clear and friendly manner, she moves her hand upward and backward to direct Joram's head. Then she immediately relaxes her hand again, and Joram comes to a halt.

*Joram wants to know whether he has done something right. Maria says, "Yes, good boy, that was right, thank you!"*

# Grooming and TTouch

If there is one thing Joram can't stand it is being brushed roughly or in a hurry. Joram wants Maria to pay full attention to him when she is grooming him. He likes it when Maria looks at the expression on his face—since he can't talk, this is his only way of showing her what he likes. Joram appreciates it when Maria's hands know to treat his body in a very special way.

At first, Joram was afraid when Maria came to groom him. Other people had sometimes been rough and impatient, yelling at him while brushing him. Joram doesn't like hard brushes. Maria takes a soft brush and places it gently and at an angle on Joram's coat. She begins to brush him with long, firm strokes. Joram's expression says, "Everything is good, Maria!" His ears and muzzle are relaxed and his head is lowered.

*Maria lets her warm hands glide flat over Joram's body. Angie calls that TTouch "Noah's March." Imagine that Maria's hands are like Noah from the story in the Bible, and he is wandering over Joram's body searching carefully for animals to put in his ark.*

Maria strokes Joram with her warm hands and in her mind, she asks, "What do you like, Joram?" Maria's hands are "awake." They sense the muscles on Joram's neck, back, and croup (the word for the horse's rear end). When Joram is hurting somewhere, these muscles try to "push the pain away" by tensing up. And when Joram is afraid, these muscles become tense so he is ready to defend himself, or run away from danger. But when Joram is happy, these muscles feel loose and relaxed.

Maria can sense how Joram is feeling and that he may be a little bit afraid. Joram is happy with Maria's hands on his body: He lowers his head and breaths out deeply. It sounds like he is making a relaxed sigh. Joram likes his human friend because she listens to him, and senses and understands how he feels.

Angie explains, "When your horse is afraid, he raises his head. He is alert and ready to flee. If you can get your horse to lower his head, he can calm down again and listen to you." Maria lays one hand on Joram's nose and one hand on his poll. She gently guides his head downward.

# Seeing and Feeling

Angie is cheerful, frisky, and sometimes flutters around like a whirlwind. Guardian angels are powerful creatures, even this happy little horse angel. She likes to help make the world a good place for animals, and animals really need a guardian angel, so it is good that Angie is there for them.

Many animals have kind and caring people that protect them. Other animals have a hard life. Angie does not neglect them. If an animal is alone and sad then you can be sure that Angie is on her way. Although Angie is very strong, it is sometimes hard for her to help animals because she isn't allowed to be seen and she doesn't have hands. For this reason she asks children to help her.

If you look carefully at a horse you can recognize many things that you are familiar with from your own life. You can see happiness, love, satisfaction, but also sadness, fear, and mistrust. You can often see friendship and thankfulness, and a little bit of worry.

*When Joram lifts his head high and his eyes and ears look like this, he is feeling mistrustful or worried.*

*Now he has lowered his head and his eyes are soft.*

When you are with your friends you usually know exactly what kind of mood they are in. When Olli's lips are pursed tightly together, Maria knows that something is wrong (luckily this isn't the case very often with Olli). When Joram is grumpy or frightened, he also clamps his lips together and tightens his chin. But when Joram is in a good mood, his lips are soft and relaxed and he may even let his lower lip droop down. Horses can't speak with words, but they communicate how they are feeling with gestures and facial expressions.

When your horse swishes his tail, something is annoying him, like a fly. When he suddenly lifts his head, it is a sign that he is startled or afraid. Horses love it when people understand these subtle signals.

*One of Joram's ears is pointed to listen to what is behind him, and the other one is listening to what is in front. Joram's chin is relaxed and his eyes have a soft expression. He appears interested and accepting of what Maria is doing.*

*Joram is showing curiosity. His ears are pricked forward and his nostrils are wide.*

# Leading *with a Partner*

Maria and Olli place poles and a wooden plank on the ground. Working together, Maria and Olli can more easily show Joram where they want him to go. They help Joram go straight and in the middle over the poles and "bridge."

Joram enjoys working alongside the two children. Maria and Olli get along well with each other. They always decide together where they will halt next. To halt, they just point their white wands at Joram's chest.

Maria and Olli stroke Joram's legs with their wand to encourage him to stand still with all four feet on the bridge. They practice having a light connection to Joram's halter with the lead rope. The rope shouldn't hang completely loose. With a light connection, Joram can tell when he is exactly in the middle between Maria and Olli.

*Joram is calm. If he were to spook and jump to the side, Olli would let go of the lead rope. Then Maria would guide Joram's head toward her and calm him before beginning to lead him again.*

With her little teeth, Angie grabs onto a wrinkle in Maria's shirt and pulls. "Stop it, that's annoying!" exclaims Maria. "It is just as annoying to Joram when you pull constantly on the lead rope," Angie explains. "Open your fingers on the lead rope when you are not asking Joram to do something."

Maria and Olli hold their lead rope with both hands and carry their wand in their outside hand. While leading, they keep some distance between themselves and Joram. He is supposed to stay in the middle, between them. This makes it look like the children and the lead ropes are Joram's "wings," which is why this exercise is called "Journey of the Homing Pigeon." A homing pigeon is a kind of bird that when released, always finds its way back home. When a horse is led from both sides like this, he feels very secure.

Maria has to walk very quickly around the corners in this ground exercise. She does a great job of staying even with Joram's head rather than running along behind him.

*Both children keep a light contact on the lead rope and its connection to Joram's halter.*

*They show Joram where to go by pointing the tip of their wand.*

*They also always stay even with his head. In this photo, Maria and Olli are already one step ahead of Joram, as he is just now stepping over the pole.*

19

# Riding Bareback

Angie asks, "Maria, do you want to become a good rider? If so, you must feel completely at home when on Joram's back. You need to be a part of Joram, and he should be part of you. Ride him without a saddle and feel how you belong together!"

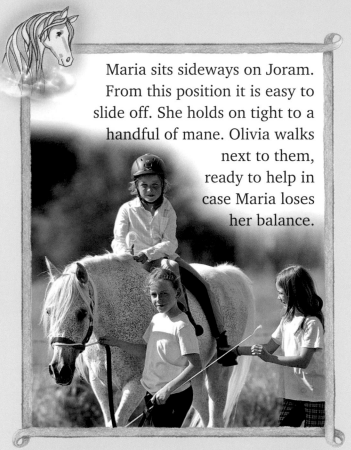

Maria sits sideways on Joram. From this position it is easy to slide off. She holds on tight to a handful of mane. Olivia walks next to them, ready to help in case Maria loses her balance.

Today school got out early, so Maria, Olli, and Olivia have extra time to spend with Joram. They take a halter, zephyr lead rope, and wand with them to the pasture. Joram comes up to them right away. He wants Maria to be a part of him!

Olli and Olivia help Maria get on Joram's back. She feels his soft, warm coat. She senses his strong back, and feels how he moves beneath her. She sits facing forward and facing backward. She sits to the side and lies on his croup.

When mounting a horse, you must be gentle and cautious. Jungle gyms are made for climbing, horses are not. Clinging to the horse or digging your knee sharply into his side will hurt him. Olli helps Maria so that this won't happen.

Olli knows how to give a "leg up." You can do this by standing right next to a horse's shoulder and supporting a friend's leg by holding her left ankle and knee. Maria counts to three out loud and pushes off the ground. With Olli's help she lifts herself onto Joram's back. Joram looks a little mistrustful at first but he stays still. He decides that the two did a good job with the leg up.

First, Maria sits forward on Joram's back. She closes her eyes. "Angie was right," she murmurs to herself, "it really does feel like I am moving with Joram's legs, or he is moving with mine."

*When Olli isn't there to give Maria a "leg up," she uses a mounting block to get on Joram. Again she is careful not to hurt Joram's back in the process.*

21

# Neck Ring and Obstacles

Today, Maria wants to see if she can ride Joram with a "neck ring." This is a stiff, adjustable circle of lariat rope that allows you to guide your horse with pressure on his neck rather than using a bridle with reins. When riding with a neck ring, you can't accidentally hurt your horse's mouth. This makes Joram happy! Olli helps at first by leading Joram with a halter and lead rope while Maria uses the neck ring to tell Joram what she would like him to do. Riding with the neck ring is fun for both Maria and Joram.

*Olli leads Joram in "Elegant Elephant" while Maria uses the neck ring to direct Joram.*

*Look how nicely Joram bends around this curve!*

Maria never pulls constantly on the neck ring. That wouldn't help Joram understand. Instead, she decides what she wants to do a few steps ahead of time and gives Joram signals with the ring on the underside of his neck. They are both familiar with these types of signals from the leading exercises they did together.

*When she is ready to halt, Maria gives a signal with the neck ring, and Olli assists with the wand on Joram's chest.*

Maria rides around obstacles—called the "Labyrinth" and the "Zigzag"—made of ground poles. She has to direct Joram clearly. To ride around a curve, Maria has to look exactly where she wants to go. She holds the neck ring with both hands and turns Joram's head and neck in the direction she wants to ride.

Joram is such a wonderful horse! He understands the neck ring so well that Olli only has to help him on occasion.

*Olli, Maria, and Joram are a good team.*

Angie loves the "Slalom" exercise! She darts around the row of cones so quickly that Maria can barely keep her in sight. Maria and Joram prefer to negotiate the cones at a steady walk. That way Joram won't knock any over. The Slalom is a great exercise because the tight turns improve a horse's flexibility.

# Riding
## with a Saddle

Maria tries to mount Joram by clinging to the stirrup and "shimmying" her way up the saddle, but Joram moves away. Angie explains, "Joram doesn't like it when you do that. If your little brother shoved and poked you, you would get out of his way, too." Remember, it is much more comfortable for a horse to be mounted with a leg up or a mounting block! After getting on, Maria gives Joram a treat. She holds it in her hand while mounting so it is ready. Angie knows that Joram will stand especially still for mounting when he is waiting for his treat.

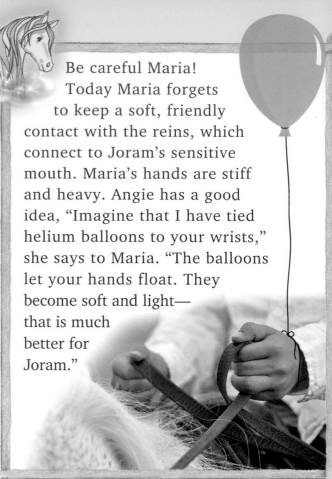

Be careful Maria! Today Maria forgets to keep a soft, friendly contact with the reins, which connect to Joram's sensitive mouth. Maria's hands are stiff and heavy. Angie has a good idea, "Imagine that I have tied helium balloons to your wrists," she says to Maria. "The balloons let your hands float. They become soft and light— that is much better for Joram."

*For added balance and security, your left hand can hold onto the mane—never the saddle. The right hand can hold onto the front, right side of the saddle.*

Maria rides at the walk. Her legs hang down relaxed and quiet and feel Joram's belly. When Maria wants to to go faster, she taps her legs softly against Joram's sides, as if she wants to "wake him up" with an almost invisible little kick. When Joram increases his pace, she immediately holds her legs quietly to show Joram that he responded correctly to her cue.

Now Maria wants to halt. Angie says, "When you approach a door that you can see is closed from a distance away, you have enough time to come to a stop before you reach it. If you just suddenly pull on Joram's mouth with the reins, it is as if you are slamming a door shut in his face! He won't be able to stop in time."

Maria takes time when preparing to halt. First, she "applies the brakes" to Joram's hind legs. She imagines that she drops a heavy ship anchor from her back and it drags along the ground while she breathes out and says a drawn-out "Whooooaaaa." She makes contact with the reins gently. Joram understands all these signals together mean he should come to a halt.

*It is easier for Joram to carry Maria when she sits up straight and in good balance.*

Maria gets help from Bibi, her riding instructor, because she is sitting somewhat slumped with her upper body. It is important that Maria stretches up tall between Bibi's two hands. Maria must stretch forward and upward as if she were a tree growing up from the ground.

*Enough for today: The stirrups are run up, the girth is loosened a hole, and Maria takes Joram's reins over his head to lead him back to the barn.*

# In the Labyrinth

Maria lays out ground poles for the exercise called the "Labyrinth" so that she and Joram can practice riding turns and curved lines. Maria must look in the direction where she wants to ride. Her body also "looks" where she wants to go by rotating in the saddle. This way, when Maria wants to turn left, Joram understands right away.

*When riding around a turn the reins should be short enough. Maria has her hands in front of the saddle as she directs Joram— that is good!*

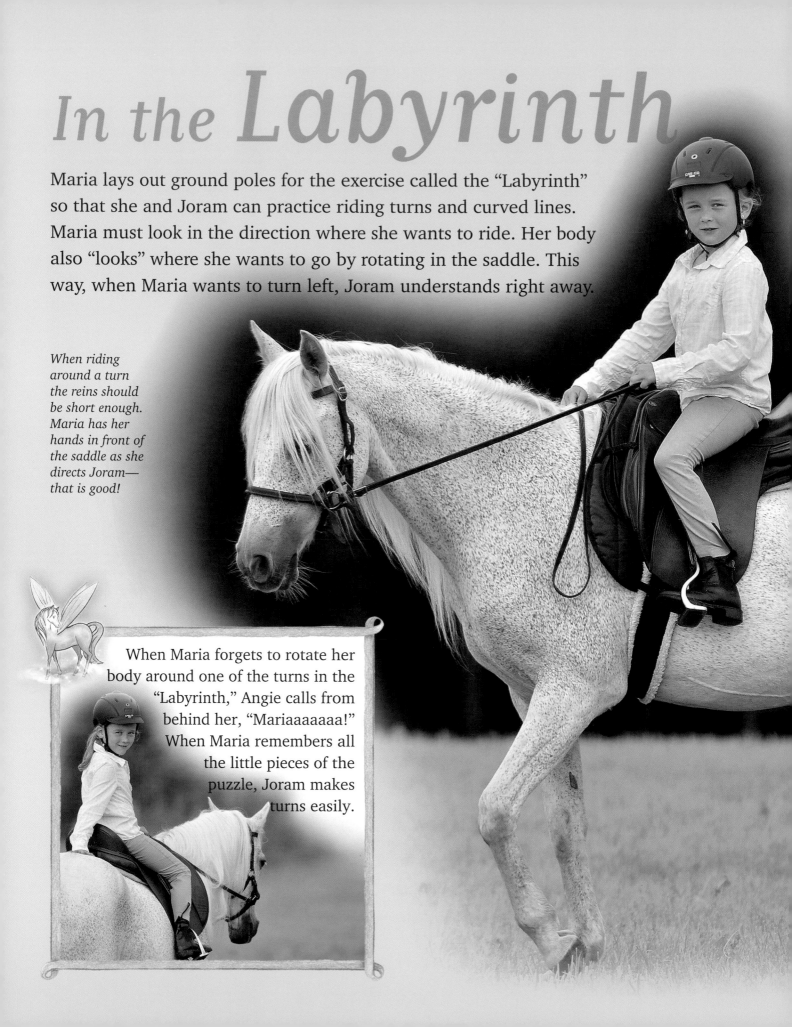

When Maria forgets to rotate her body around one of the turns in the "Labyrinth," Angie calls from behind her, "Mariaaaaaaa!" When Maria remembers all the little pieces of the puzzle, Joram makes turns easily.

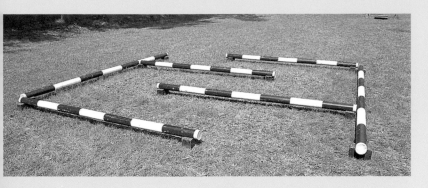

Here is an example of how you can lay out the "Labyrinth" with ground poles. The tight turns help Joram become agile and flexible. Horses are not as flexible as Joana, the cat. Horses in the wild only have to run straight ahead. It is important to have horses practice bending their body around turns and curves. There are many horses that lean to the inside of the turn, just like you would tilt when riding a bicycle around a curve. This isn't good because it is unsafe.

*Turns are very difficult—Maria, turn your body more to the left!*

*Maria and Joram complete a turn successfully!*

*Maria never forgets to tell Joram when he has been good. He loves a stroke or a pat.*

# After the Ride

Good manners and being polite is extremely important to horses. Joram doesn't like it at all when Maria tries to put his halter on without greeting him first. And he likes it when she thanks him after a ride.

Joram tries very hard to please Maria when she rides him. If Maria doesn't appreciate what he does for her, he is very sad, or resentful. Then he does not want to be ridden by Maria the next time she comes to see him. Maria never forgets to do something nice for Joram after riding. She does it because she is grateful and also because it's fun to do something for a friend.

Horses often have back pain, but they patiently carry us around anyway. Have you ever had to go for a hike or long walk with uncomfortable shoes on? That is how it feels to a horse when his saddle doesn't fit. Horses that do not like to be saddled, that nip when the girth is tightened, and that move away when the rider mounts are often trying to tell people that something is wrong with their saddle.

Even if your saddle fits your horse well, or you ride without a saddle, there are many good

*Maria "draws" a lightning bolt over and over again with her fingers in the Zigzag TTouch. Joram enjoys the feeling of being "scratched" like this.*

things that can be done for the horse's back. For example, you can do the "Zigzag TTouch" after riding.

Often you see horses grooming each other with their teeth. When Maria does the "Zigzag TTouch" on Joram, this is what it feels like to him. This TTouch is like a sign of friendship between them. Maria strokes Joram as if she was drawing a lightning bolt over and over again across his whole body.

*Maria can tell by Joram's facial expression that he likes the lukewarm water she's using to bathe him after their ride.*

Angie gives Maria another tip for "thanking" Joram after a ride: "Glide your fingers gently down strands of Joram's mane," she says. "You can do this with his tail too. He loves it!"

Today, Joram worked hard. He is sweaty under the saddle and on the girth area. Maria uses a sponge and lukewarm water to sponge him off. Joram is extremely sensitive to water. (After all, he is an Arabian from the desert!) Sometimes when the sweat has already dried on Joram's body, Maria uses a soft brush to clean his coat.

Before Maria goes home she lays her hand on Joram's head and says, "Thank you, I will see you tomorrow."

*Maria cleans up manure in the pasture so Joram has a nice, clean place to relax after their ride.*

29

# Parts of the Horse

Today Maria has some things to do after school. She doesn't have much time in the afternoon to work with Joram. Angie says that hurrying and horses don't go well together. Horses always have time for you. They don't understand when you want them to hurry up because you don't have time for them. When short on time, it is better to do something other than riding. So Maria makes herself cozy at home. She has a photograph of Joram and decides to learn the names of the parts of the horse.

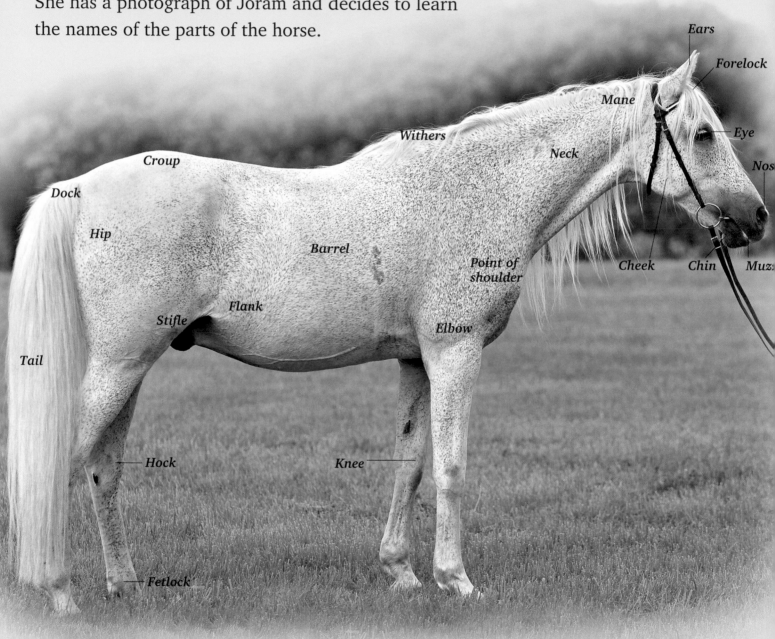

Ears

Forelock

Mane

Withers

Eye

Neck

Croup

Nos

Dock

Hip

Barrel

Point of shoulder

Cheek

Chin

Muzz

Flank

Stifle

Elbow

Tail

Hock

Knee

Fetlock

# Goodbye!

Joram isn't just a made-up character in this book; he is a real horse. Maria, Olli, and Olivia are real children, as well.

Joram is truly a wonderful horse. There are many people in his life that love him very much. He was born and grew up in the wild. That is why he used to be a very shy horse. During the first year of his life no one could get close enough to touch him.

When Joram came to live with me I had to handle him very carefully. Luckily I had already learned a lot from Linda Tellington-Jones. Everything that I have explained to you in this book played a role in making Joram the wonderful friend he is today. The Tellington Method has helped horses like him all over the world gain trust in people.

Whether Angie, our guardian of animals, is real, you have to decide for yourself. Can you see her? You just have to clear your mind of all thoughts...

*Many thanks to...*

✭ *Linda Tellington-Jones: The world famous horse trainer who has brought us TTouches and many great training ideas. She advocates that people treat animals in a conscientious and gentle manner.*

✭ *Maria, Olli, Olivia, and Joram, the Arabian gelding.*

✭ *Horst Streitferdt: The photographer who took the wonderful photos for this book.*

✭ *Petra Eimer: The illustrator who drew the pictures of Angie.*

✭ *Sigrid Walter: The graphic designer who did the page layout.*

✭ *Angie: The "guardian" angel of animals.*

**For more information about TTouch and the Tellington Method, for both children and adults, contact:**

**Tellington TTouch Training**
**866.4.TTOUCH**
**www.ttouch.com**

**ALSO RECOMMENDED:**

**The Ultimate**
**Horse Behavior and Training Book**
*Enlightened and Revolutionary Solutions*
*for the 21st Century*
Linda Tellington-Jones
with Bobbie Jo Liebermann